Always tell people the nice things you think about them.

Be yourself, unapologetically

Under the surface of your life is something beautiful. And just like the ocean, the scariest part is you don't know what's down there

Poems That Were Written On Trains But Weren't Written About Trains

Daragh Fleming

Poems That Were Written On Trains But Weren't
Written About Trains
Copyright © 2022
DARK THIRTY POETRY PUBLISHING
ISBN: 978-1-7397975-3-9

All Rights Reserved

First edition

Artwork by

DTPP4

DARK THIRTY POETRY PUBLISHING

Other titles by the author:

The Book of Revelations (Riversong Books, 2019)

If You Are Reading This Then Drink Water (Riversong Books, 2020)

Notes For A Mid-Youth Crisis (Bottlecap Press, 2022)

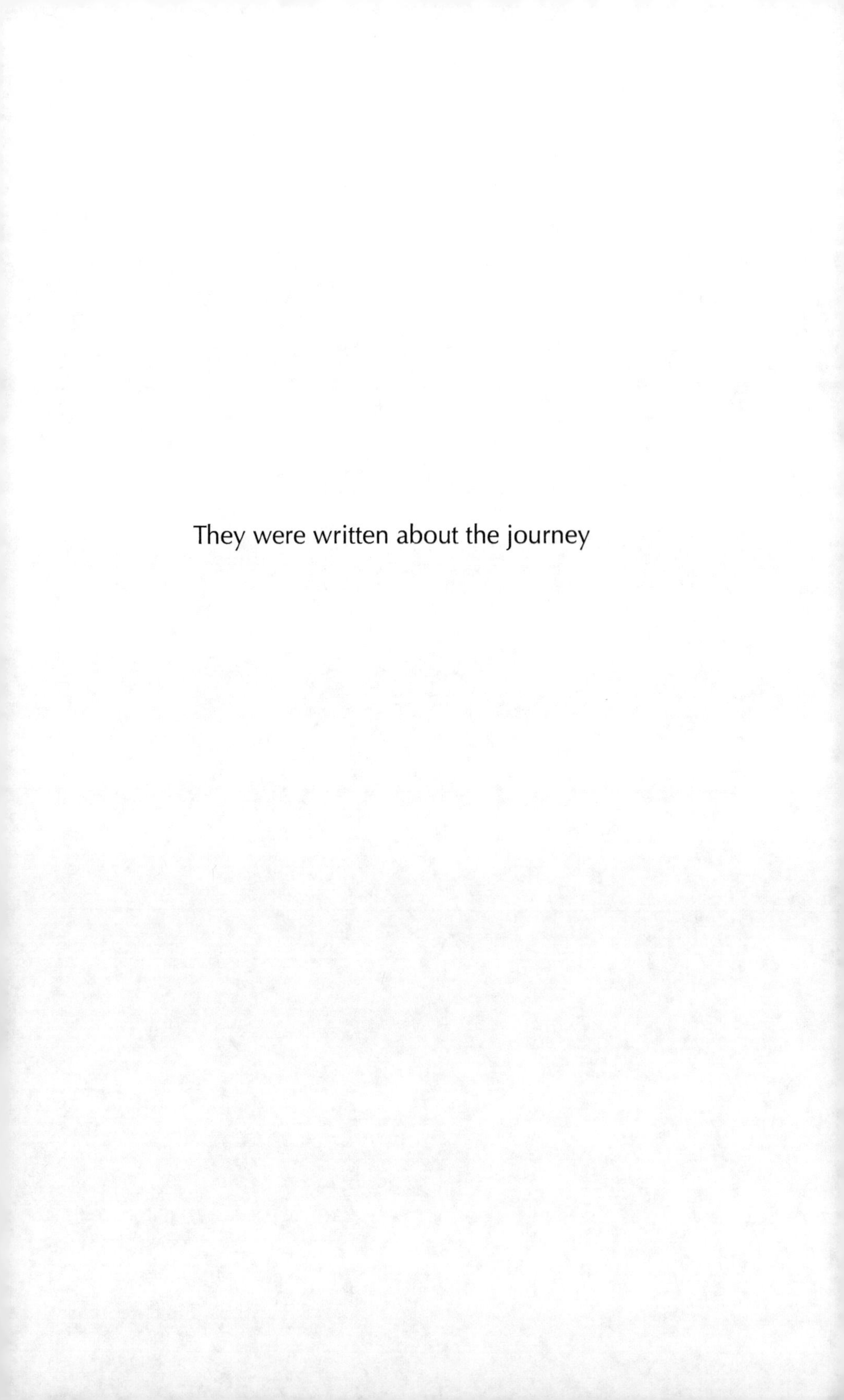

They were written about the journey

Dedication
For Sylvia and Séamus

I Did A Cannonball Off The Deep End

Parc Güell in the rain seemed like an activity for a
sunny day,
nine thousand and two unread emails,
is that a sign of a life in neglect?
Or a life in its prime.

There is no smell of heat here, and I have no flowery
shirts.
Suddenly it no longer feels foreign,
except for the language which I cannot speak.

Jumping in the deep end head first is safer than doing
anything
similar in the shallow end of the pool,
assuming you know how to swim.

Dondé Está La Cerveza?

you'd imagine a fella would try to learn the
language instead of stumbling around as if
in the dark. The few words known sticking to
lips like glue with a look of pure confusion
on the faces of all participants.
Most languages, you'll surely know,
were not designed to be spoken in an Irish
accent. Just point us towards the nearest
bar, so we can sit quietly and sip from
the few words we do know as we
ponder our own mortification.

8 Minutes Before The Train From Barcelona To Lyon On A Monday

In
the city of dogs
I swear that a magpie
followed me here from home,
it hopped and skipped around our feet
and we threw gorgeous thick breadcrumbs to it
while an older man with leather skin took its picture.
Pictures of a bird considered a pest in the countries it
comes from,
and it struck me then how exotic is simply a subjective
form of adoration;
and how there is wonder right in front of you and I in
this moment right now.
It is there if you and I could only open our eyes to the
world and see it earnestly,
the eternal wonder and magic to be found in something
as mundane as a black & white magpie.

My Favourite Thing About Venice

My favourite thing about Venice is
already clear despite never having been there,
it is not the canals or the Rialto, or the gondolas,
it is not the food, or the culture or the islands.
My favourite thing about Venice is
her – her accent and the way she smiles,
the way she says my name
while squeezing my hand in hers,
and how she says she hates me
but really means something contrasting.
I've never been there, but
my favourite thing about Venice is her.

The Train To Berlin, November 5th

I wrote to October for patience
that I might lullaby a sense of self
from weeks full of decades,
the voice of autumn is quiet but
full of ignored importance.
Do you feel the dreaded longing
for the ocean at night?

That is the call of November,
it whispers through the rain
and tells deadly lies.
October never returned my letters,
and as I waited and waited,
I realised my request was answered
in those long weeks between the ends
of months.

Half-dose Of Fun In A Nameless Bar

The air is fuzzy now
it is fun! it is fun!
I can breathe underwater,
and I have never loved strangers
so genuinely;
do you feel like you have
superpowers too?
It certainly is fun,
and I wonder whether
I'll ever be able to bend my knees again.
On the road that borders fear,
along the edge of joy
I became awake before
I woke up tomorrow.

An Accidental Cruise Ship From Stockholm To Helsinki

Under the surface of your life is something beautiful,
and just like the ocean the scariest part is
you don't know what's down there.

What's Your Favourite Colour?

The rich and intense familiar purples of
sadness are upon me in an
unfamiliar shape
new reasons emerge now
sadness – not because I cannot have you
sadness because I have to let you go
I thought these days would
bleed on for eternity
but they passed as quickly as any
other four days I've had
on the second last night you
cooked for me the food of your
culture and I thought a hundred times
to tell you that I loved you
but I never did.

The 11:22 To Budapest

The train has just now pulled away from Bratislava. I only got to catch a glimpse. I keep falling asleep, but then my head drops causing me to awaken again like someone who is falling out of bed during the fitful night. A familiar sadness sits next to me, asking questions about where we're going, and why I am currently 26 years and 363 days old skirting the borders of Austria and Slovakia. Other passengers have come and gone from compartment five of coach 368, but I have remained. I am here for the long haul, breaching the night on a train forged from silver sunlight and there are things to be talked about but there is no rush to do it just yet.

I Missed A Train To Katowice

Under slept with damp armpits
a Turkish man converses with me,
despite a lack of understanding.
The walls are closing in
as we slip across snow-covered fields
in undistinguished parts of vague
country borders.

I cannot for the life of me remember
who I was even just three months ago,
when I was well-slept and too comfortable
to even be alive. A limitless life has
revealed the limitations of a life I no
longer want. You cannot live openly in
a box shut tight. Assuming I make the
next train I'll sleep in Krakow tonight.

Layover In Bohumin I think

A couple chats beside
me. She ends up paying
for their coffees after
a brief debate
"tell me what it costs in euros"
we're not in Europe anymore
well, we sort of are
are they leaving already?
I've been here for ages
writing about people
behind their backs.

13:34 Direct To Poznan

I have come to the conclusion after
far too many nights of drunken sin
that you do not have me fully, nor
forever. I am recklessly evasive and
have never existed any differently.
I will hurt you.
This is inevitable.
It will hurtle through
the darkness, a highspeed terror aimed
at you, simply because I cannot control
the urge to look elsewhere for love.

A Very Slow Train From Venice To Verona

red wine.
When will I admit that my liver drowns in
red wine.
Because I'm afraid to face myself without
red wine.
There's a monster here. I can feel it clawing through the
red wine.
I can feel its thirst to hurt and fuck and lie despite the
red wine.
And so I try to drown it with all this
red wine.

The Rhine

I thought about it.
Throwing myself into the river

I thought about doing it.
Not because I wanted to die

But because I wanted to hurt you.
I wanted you to hurt

And I thought throwing myself in the river
Would be the most effective way to do it

I stared at the railing for a lifetime.
But I didn't do it

Because it would have been too cold
and I would have been dead.

The Reasons This Wasn't Love

It was on a Monday night in Berlin during
December when my heart gave up and I
died inside a pint glass in a hostel, not far
from the river between the S-Bahn station
and a Christmas market where tourists
shopped for late presents, and drank hot
wine as the bitter wind glazed in over the
water like the icy breath of a great and
terrifying bird. Causing the gloveless
hands of children to turn red before it
turned up in my face as I stood against it
leaning on the hostel's wall, and wondered,
 why you betrayed me and why I'd lied to
you before I turned again and lost my
thoughts in another pint, and smiled
at another girl and failed to change once again.

The First Man To Buy You Flowers

The first man to buy you flowers
was also the last one who loved you,
he was the one who lied to you
and the one who let you slip away.

The first man to buy you flowers
was also the one who was reckless with your heart,
he's the one whose journal you opened
to read sins that ripped us both apart.

The Voldemort Conundrum

There is a part of you
entwined with a part of me,
a subconscious
feather-like connection
which may kill us both
if we prolong our intention
to leave it unaddressed.

Home

Leave home to find it,
the part that is missing
on the path, along the way
you will see
the beauty of your life
is clearest from afar.

The Delayed 10:20 From Bergamo To Dublin

I'd never seen the Alps before and I've
never met so many people who I'll miss
so dearly, and likely never see again.
Stretched out across the map of the world
and of my life like great interlinking river
networks, all flowing pure and imperfect
and magic. Complicated yet simple.
Heartbreak doesn't require time.
Heartbreak requires only feeling. Feelings
deep as bottomless wells. Feelings I could
never feel before, now rush through me like
the roaring rapids of those rivers and I render
myself glad to find tears because it means
I'm alive. I'm alive, and well, and
heartbroken, and I've seen the Alps now
the same way a God must see them. Love
has never needed time to grow. Love only
needs you to give everything without fear.

Acknowledgements:

This collection was written during a very tumultuous and exciting trip around Europe, and so many of the people I met along the way are owed gratitude for their influence upon this collection. In particular, to Caterina, who was the muse for many of them. To my parents, brother, friends, and family, as always none of this work is possible without your continued support and encouragement. To Sylvia and Séamus, two important people I met along the way, thank you for your generosity of friendship. To Adam, my editor, thank you for taking the time to read, and polish my work, and thank you also for publishing it. And finally to the many, many, many unnamed friends I met and got to know in Europe, thank you for making this time in my life a very special one.

Daragh Fleming is an author from Cork in Ireland who uses a conversational style to delve into complex themes which emerge in everyday life. He has two collections of short stories published by Riversong Books; The Book of Revelations (2019) and If You Are Reading This Then Drink Water (2020). Recently he was the winner of the Cork Arts 'From The Well' Short Story Competition. His most recent story features in Époque Press' é-zine. His debut chapbook, Notes For a Mid-Youth Crisis, is launching in February 2022 with Bottlecap Press. His non-fiction mental health book, Lonely Boy, is being published by BookHub Publishing later in 2022.

RELEASED BY DARK THIRTY POETRY

ANTHOLOGY ONE
THIS ISN'T WHY WE'RE HERE
MORTAL BEINGS
POEMS THAT WERE WRITTEN ON TRAINS BUT
WEREN'T WRITTEN ABOUT TRAINS